manifest
•*ish*

manifest
·ish

Manifest·ish
Copyright © 2020 by Shaun Marie

First edition

For information about special discounts for bulk purchases,
please contact H. Trinity Enterprises, LLC at htrinityenterprises@gmail.com.

Cover artwork concept by Paula McDade. Art direction
and book layout by Shaun Marie for H. Trinity Enterprises, LLC.

ISBN 9798649347273
Manufactured in the United States of America

manifest
·ish

This Journal is dedicated to:

You :)

Whether you are a Christian who believes in The Holy Trinity of God, you believe in a higher being, other religious relationship, or the Universe, etc., He/it has all power and has given you authority to exercise within God's power. Within this power, love is the greatest energy source that you could practice or exude. In knowing that, why would you not specifically move to operate in the power you were given at its highest, love. Think about it. Do not lose focus on what we're doing here. Wherever I have written the word "God" in this text, if your higher power is something or someone else, replace the noun for that which fits you.

Let's be clear. Success is not always defined as material success. Good things that come to you do not always have to be materialistic things. Sometimes one seeks a closer relationship with their God, good health, peace, joy, happiness or positive relationships.

You must change the way you think and feel to change your life.

Everything in your life revolves around two things...positivity or negativity. Likewise, when manifesting, EVERYTHING is revolved around either a positive force or negative force. Love, life and good are associated with positivity. Hate, death and bad is associated with negativity. Everything else between love and hate matter as well.

Life and death are in the power of the tongue. Whatever you put out into the universe will return to you.

"People who have great lives think and talk about what they love, more than what they don't love and people who are struggling think and talk about what they don't love, more than what they do love." ~Rhonda Byrne, Author of The Power

Let's look at some words and thoughts and what they are associated with.

Positive	Negative
love	*hate*
good	*bad*
acceptable	*unacceptable*
excellent	*lousy*
favorable	*dumb*
marvelous	*stupid*
valuable	*failure*
wonderful	*horrible*
worth	*unworthy*
free	*slave*
easy	*hard*
beautiful	*ugly*
do	*don't*
can	*can't*
win	*lose*
is	*isn't*
life	*death*

"Be careful of your moods and feelings, for there is an unbroken connection between your feelings and your visible world."

"Become aware of what you are thinking and you will recognize a law between your mood and your surrounding circumstances."

"The law operates by faith. If you believe, no effort is necessary to see the fulfillment of your every desire." ~Neville Goddard, Spiritual Philosopher

Get the idea?

What is Manifesting?

The dictionary definition is: *verb (used with object) to make clear or evident to the eye or the understanding; show plainly or to show something clearly, through signs or actions.* However, in this sense, the law of attractions defines manifesting as putting something into your physical reality through thought, feeling and beliefs; intentionally creating what you want.

What is The Law of Attraction?

The law of attraction is the belief that the universe creates and provides infinitely for you that which your thoughts are focused on, whether positive or negative.

It doesn't matter where you are in your life right now, where you came from or how you used to think about your life and what led you to this point, YOU have the power and authority to change your circumstances, your reality and live out your best life (without having to go back and forth with anybody 😉).

Are you still following where we are going with all of this?

Like attracts like. What this means is the results of positive thoughts are positive outcomes. As well, negative thoughts produce results of negative outcomes. For instance, when you have a bad day, do not talk about it, as the more you talk about it the more you think about it and are putting negative words and thoughts into the universe. Find something, because there is ALWAYS something, good from that day and talk about that.

You must do whatever it takes to keep your energy positive. Do something that makes you happier. For me, I listen to my favorite 90's R&B songs or maybe some high energy club music that I used to listen to and have fun with my friends while listening to it, when we were in our 20's. For you it may be journaling, taking a walk, watching a funny movie (laughter always puts us in a better mood), or having quality time with your family. Again, you must keep your energy and vibe positive and on a good frequency.

Here are some thoughts about manifesting money into your life:

"Limited and negative thinking leads to limited action, or even counterproductive action, and produces negative results. If you have the negative thought, "Money is the root of all evil" it is not likely that you'll take action that would lead to your financial success, given you have such negative associations with money. After all, why would you want to be evil? In fact, if you do happen to effortlessly attract money, you'll probably fritter it away. The first step to attracting wealth is to eliminate the negative beliefs you have. The next step is to replace those with positive beliefs and then work to make that new positive belief feel real to you by cementing it with action. For example, you might open a savings account and every week deposit $100 while saying, "I'm effortlessly growing my wealth." It helps to remember that money is neither good nor evil, but simply a tool that can be used to create good in the world. You can use a hammer to build a house or you can use a hammer to clock someone on the head. Try not to blame the tool."

~Talane Miedaner, author and life coach

I must warn you, if you are not a giving person nor wish to become a giving person, manifesting good things will not work for you. God loves a cheerful giver. This is not just related to money. There are so many ways to give in a positive sense. Giving can take place by giving love to someone, words of encouragement, time, attention, volunteering, donating, etc.

When you desire something good for your life you must think about, speak about and feel about it with positive thoughts, with all your being. It is extremely easy to fall into negative thinking and throw what God and the universe has for you off course. Remember, you must believe what you are seeking is coming to you with all your might. Some things will manifest themselves into your life quickly and others may take some time, as God and the universe has to move things in and out of your path for the good things to reach you as they are meant to be. Do not ever give up on believing for what you want, NO MATTER WHAT.

Over the next three months, you will journal words, thoughts and desires. If manifesting is new to you, at first, you may not feel the power of it. As you continue with journaling consistently, you will start to feel the changes coming into your life, as ultimately, they will. Realize that there will be times wherein God is just so good that He gives you better than what you asked and believed for.

Stay positive, stay blessed and keep it Manifest-ish!

Vision - Write it and Make it Plain!
Goals for anytime between now & 5 years in the future.

Vision - See it Before You See it!
In-Journal Vision Board
Tape, Glue, Staple or draw images, graphics or words that support what you want.

On This Day...

Example

Example

Date: 5/23/20

I Am Grateful For:

Waking up this morning. Thank you!

The awesome day I had yesterday

My health

My family

Being able to bless others

My home

> There is **ALWAYS** something to be grateful for everyday. Some days you might write the same things as yesterday and other days you may not. Challenge yourself to find one thing different to be grateful for daily. Before you know it, you will be a champ at showing gratitude!

I Affirm That I:

Today is a great day!

I am beautiful

I am powerful

I am worthy

I am happy with my life

I am all that I need to be

I am a boss!

I enjoy abundance for myself and family

I let go of any and all negativity

God/The universe is working for my good!

> **DO NOT** write anything negative about yourself, anything or anyone. **POSITIVE** affirmations **ONLY** (even if you don't fully feel or see it yet!)

Goal(s) For the Day

Organize pantry

read and clear email inbox

start reading a book

NOTES:

read a good quote:
Start each day with
a positive thought
and a grateful heart.
- Roy T. Bennett

today was such a good day! :)

On This Day...

Date:

I Am Grateful For:

I Affirm That I:

Goal(s) For the Day

NOTES:

On This Day...

Date:

I Am Grateful For:

I Affirm That I:

Goal(s) For the Day

NOTES:

On This Day...

Date:

I Am Grateful For:

I Affirm That I:

Goal(s) For the Day

NOTES:

On This Day...

Date:

I Am Grateful For:

I Affirm That I:

Goal(s) For the Day

NOTES:

On This Day...

Date:

I Am Grateful For:

I Affirm That I:

Goal(s) For the Day

NOTES:

On This Day...

Date:

I Am Grateful For:

I Affirm That I:

Goal(s) For the Day

NOTES:

On This Day...

Date:

I Am Grateful For:

I Affirm That I:

Goal(s) For the Day

NOTES:

On This Day...

Date:

I Am Grateful For:

I Affirm That I:

Goal(s) For the Day

NOTES:

On This Day...

Date:

I Am Grateful For:

I Affirm That I:

Goal(s) For the Day

NOTES:

On This Day...

Date:

I Am Grateful For:

I Affirm That I:

Goal(s) For the Day

NOTES:

On This Day...

I Am Grateful For:

I Affirm That I:

Goal(s) For the Day

NOTES:

On This Day...

Date:

I Am Grateful For:

I Affirm That I:

Goal(s) For the Day

NOTES:

On This Day...

Date:

I Am Grateful For:

I Affirm That I:

Goal(s) For the Day

NOTES:

On This Day...

Date:

I Am Grateful For:

I Affirm That I:

Goal(s) For the Day

NOTES:

On This Day...

Date:

I Am Grateful For:

I Affirm That I:

Goal(s) For the Day

NOTES:

On This Day...

Date:

I Am Grateful For:

I Affirm That I:

Goal(s) For the Day

NOTES:

On This Day...

Date:

I Am Grateful For:

I Affirm That I:

Goal(s) For the Day

NOTES:

On This Day...

Date:

I Am Grateful For:

I Affirm That I:

Goal(s) For the Day

NOTES:

On This Day...

Date:

I Am Grateful For:

I Affirm That I:

Goal(s) For the Day

NOTES:

On This Day...

Date:

I Am Grateful For:

I Affirm That I:

Goal(s) For the Day

NOTES:

On This Day...

Date:

I Am Grateful For:

I Affirm That I:

Goal(s) For the Day

NOTES:

On This Day...

Date:

I Am Grateful For:

I Affirm That I:

Goal(s) For the Day

NOTES:

On This Day...

Date:

I Am Grateful For:

I Affirm That I:

Goal(s) For the Day

NOTES:

On This Day...

Date:

I Am Grateful For:

I Affirm That I:

Goal(s) For the Day

NOTES:

On This Day...

Date:

I Am Grateful For:

I Affirm That I:

Goal(s) For the Day

NOTES:

On This Day...

Date:

I Am Grateful For:

I Affirm That I:

Goal(s) For the Day

NOTES:

On This Day...

Date:

I Am Grateful For:

I Affirm That I:

Goal(s) For the Day

NOTES:

On This Day...

Date:

I Am Grateful For:

I Affirm That I:

Goal(s) For the Day

NOTES:

On This Day...

Date:

I Am Grateful For:

I Affirm That I:

Goal(s) For the Day

NOTES:

On This Day...

Date:

I Am Grateful For:

I Affirm That I:

Goal(s) For the Day

NOTES:

On This Day...

Date:

I Am Grateful For:

I Affirm That I:

Goal(s) For the Day

NOTES:

Monthly Recap

Record some of the good things that happened to you this past month.
Remember some of the goals that you absolutely smashed and don't forget those things
that came into "Manifest-Ish" this month too!

On This Day...

Date:

I Am Grateful For:

I Affirm That I:

Goal(s) For the Day

NOTES:

On This Day...

Date:

I Am Grateful For:

I Affirm That I:

Goal(s) For the Day

NOTES:

On This Day...

Date:

I Am Grateful For:

I Affirm That I:

Goal(s) For the Day

NOTES:

On This Day...

Date:

I Am Grateful For:

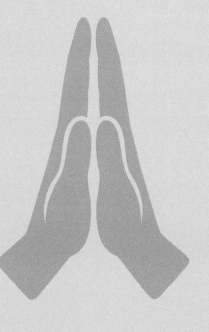

I Affirm That I:

Goal(s) For the Day

NOTES:

On This Day...

Date:

I Am Grateful For:

I Affirm That I:

Goal(s) For the Day

NOTES:

On This Day...

Date:

I Am Grateful For:

I Affirm That I:

Goal(s) For the Day

NOTES:

On This Day...

Date:

I Am Grateful For:

I Affirm That I:

Goal(s) For the Day

NOTES:

On This Day...

Date:

I Am Grateful For:

I Affirm That I:

Goal(s) For the Day

NOTES:

On This Day...

Date:

I Am Grateful For:

I Affirm That I:

Goal(s) For the Day

NOTES:

On This Day...

Date:

I Am Grateful For:

I Affirm That I:

Goal(s) For the Day

NOTES:

On This Day...

Date:

I Am Grateful For:

I Affirm That I:

Goal(s) For the Day

NOTES:

On This Day...

Date:

I Am Grateful For:

I Affirm That I:

Goal(s) For the Day

NOTES:

On This Day...

Date:

I Am Grateful For:

I Affirm That I:

Goal(s) For the Day

NOTES:

On This Day...

Date:

I Am Grateful For:

I Affirm That I:

Goal(s) For the Day

NOTES:

On This Day...

I Am Grateful For:

I Affirm That I:

Goal(s) For the Day

NOTES:

On This Day...

Date:

I Am Grateful For:

I Affirm That I:

Goal(s) For the Day

NOTES:

On This Day...

Date:

I Am Grateful For:

I Affirm That I:

Goal(s) For the Day

NOTES:

On This Day...

Date:

I Am Grateful For:

I Affirm That I:

Goal(s) For the Day

NOTES:

On This Day...

Date:

I Am Grateful For:

I Affirm That I:

Goal(s) For the Day

NOTES:

On This Day...

Date:

I Am Grateful For:

I Affirm That I:

Goal(s) For the Day

NOTES:

On This Day...

Date:

I Am Grateful For:

I Affirm That I:

Goal(s) For the Day

NOTES:

On This Day...

Date:

I Am Grateful For:

I Affirm That I:

Goal(s) For the Day

NOTES:

On This Day...

Date:

I Am Grateful For:

I Affirm That I:

Goal(s) For the Day

NOTES:

On This Day...

Date:

I Am Grateful For:

I Affirm That I:

Goal(s) For the Day

NOTES:

On This Day...

Date:

I Am Grateful For:

I Affirm That I:

Goal(s) For the Day

NOTES:

On This Day...

Date:

I Am Grateful For:

I Affirm That I:

Goal(s) For the Day

NOTES:

On This Day...

Date:

I Am Grateful For:

I Affirm That I:

Goal(s) For the Day

NOTES:

On This Day...

Date:

I Am Grateful For:

I Affirm That I:

Goal(s) For the Day

NOTES:

On This Day...

Date:

I Am Grateful For:

I Affirm That I:

Goal(s) For the Day

NOTES:

On This Day...

Date:

I Am Grateful For:

I Affirm That I:

Goal(s) For the Day

NOTES:

On This Day...

Date:

I Am Grateful For:

I Affirm That I:

Goal(s) For the Day

NOTES:

Monthly Recap

Record some of the good things that happened to you this past month.
Remember some of the goals that you absolutely smashed and don't forget those things
that came into "Manifest-Ish" this month too!

On This Day...

Date:

I Am Grateful For:

I Affirm That I:

Goal(s) For the Day

NOTES:

On This Day...

Date:

I Am Grateful For:

I Affirm That I:

Goal(s) For the Day

NOTES:

On This Day...

Date:

I Am Grateful For:

I Affirm That I:

Goal(s) For the Day

NOTES:

On This Day...

Date:

I Am Grateful For:

I Affirm That I:

Goal(s) For the Day

NOTES:

On This Day...

Date:

I Am Grateful For:

I Affirm That I:

Goal(s) For the Day

NOTES:

On This Day...

Date:

I Am Grateful For:

I Affirm That I:

Goal(s) For the Day

NOTES:

On This Day...

Date:

I Am Grateful For:

I Affirm That I:

Goal(s) For the Day

NOTES:

On This Day...

Date:

I Am Grateful For:

I Affirm That I:

Goal(s) For the Day

NOTES:

On This Day...

Date:

I Am Grateful For:

I Affirm That I:

Goal(s) For the Day

NOTES:

On This Day...

Date:

I Am Grateful For:

I Affirm That I:

Goal(s) For the Day

NOTES:

On This Day...

Date:

I Am Grateful For:

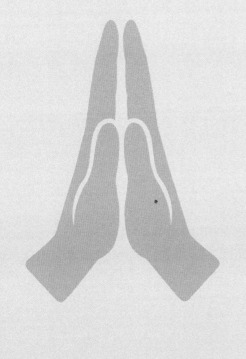

I Affirm That I:

Goal(s) For the Day

NOTES:

On This Day...

Date:

I Am Grateful For:

I Affirm That I:

Goal(s) For the Day

NOTES:

On This Day...

Date:

I Am Grateful For:

I Affirm That I:

Goal(s) For the Day

NOTES:

On This Day...

Date:

I Am Grateful For:

I Affirm That I:

Goal(s) For the Day

NOTES:

On This Day...

Date:

I Am Grateful For:

I Affirm That I:

Goal(s) For the Day

NOTES:

On This Day...

Date:

I Am Grateful For:

I Affirm That I:

Goal(s) For the Day

NOTES:

On This Day...

Date:

I Am Grateful For:

I Affirm That I:

Goal(s) For the Day

NOTES:

On This Day...

I Am Grateful For:

I Affirm That I:

Goal(s) For the Day

NOTES:

On This Day...

Date:

I Am Grateful For:

I Affirm That I:

Goal(s) For the Day

NOTES:

On This Day...

Date:

I Am Grateful For:

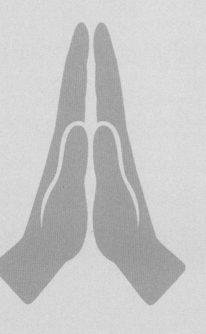

I Affirm That I:

Goal(s) For the Day

NOTES:

On This Day...

Date:

I Am Grateful For:

I Affirm That I:

Goal(s) For the Day

NOTES:

On This Day...

Date:

I Am Grateful For:

I Affirm That I:

Goal(s) For the Day

NOTES:

On This Day...

Date:

I Am Grateful For:

I Affirm That I:

Goal(s) For the Day

NOTES:

On This Day...

Date:

I Am Grateful For:

I Affirm That I:

Goal(s) For the Day

NOTES:

On This Day...

Date:

I Am Grateful For:

I Affirm That I:

Goal(s) For the Day

NOTES:

On This Day...

Date:

I Am Grateful For:

I Affirm That I:

Goal(s) For the Day

NOTES:

On This Day...

Date:

I Am Grateful For:

I Affirm That I:

Goal(s) For the Day

NOTES:

On This Day...

Date:

I Am Grateful For:

I Affirm That I:

Goal(s) For the Day

NOTES:

On This Day...

Date:

I Am Grateful For:

I Affirm That I:

Goal(s) For the Day

NOTES:

On This Day...

Date:

I Am Grateful For:

I Affirm That I:

Goal(s) For the Day

NOTES:

On This Day...

Date:

I Am Grateful For:

I Affirm That I:

Goal(s) For the Day

NOTES:

Monthly Recap

Record some of the good things that happened to you this past month.
Remember some of the goals that you absolutely smashed and don't forget those things
that came into "Manifest-Ish" this month too!

Made in the USA
Columbia, SC
15 January 2021